WORD PROBLEMS
USING
FRACTIONS

MASTERING MATH WORD PROBLEMS

Zella Williams and
Rebecca Wingard-Nelson

Enslow Publishing
101 W. 23rd Street
Suite 240
New York, NY 10011
USA

enslow.com

Published in 2017 by Enslow Publishing, LLC.
101 W. 23rd Street, Suite 240, New York, NY 10011

Library of Congress Cataloging-in-Publication Data

Names: Williams, Zella, author. | Wingard-Nelson, Rebecca, author.
Title: Word problems using fractions / Zella Williams and Rebecca Wingard-Nelson.
Description: New York, NY : Enslow Publishing, 2017. | Series: Mastering math word problems | Includes bibliographical references and index.
Identifiers: LCCN 2016032319| ISBN 9780766082625 (library bound) | ISBN 9780766082618 (6 pack) | ISBN 9780766082601 (pbk.)
Subjects: LCSH: Fractions—Juvenile literature. | Word problems (Mathematics)—Juvenile literature.
Classification: LCC QA117 .W56775 2016 | DDC 513.2/6—dc23
LC record available at https://lccn.loc.gov/2016032319

Printed in China

To Our Readers: We have done our best to make sure all websites in this book were active and appropriate when we went to press. However, the author and the publisher have no control over and assume no liability for the material available on those websites or on any websites they may link to. Any comments or suggestions can be sent by e-mail to customerservice@enslow.com.

Portions of this book originally appeared in the book *Fun Food Word Problems Starring Fractions*.

Photo Credits: Cover, p. 1 Paul Bradbury/OJO Images/Getty Images; pp. 3, 36 Alena Ozerova/Shutterstock.com; p. 4 Huntstock/Getty Images; p. 5 (book) Maximilian Laschon/Shutterstock.com; p. 7 Tanya Constantine/Blend Images/Getty Images; p. 10 Tetra Images/Getty Images; p. 12 Muriel de Seze/DigitalVision/Getty Images; p. 14 JGI/Jamie Grill/Blend Images/Getty Images; p. 16 ©iStockphoto.com/bhofack2; p. 18 ajafoto/iStock/Thinkstock; p. 20 Hemera Technologies/Photos.com/Thinkstock; p. 22 Marie C Fields/Shutterstock.com; p. 24 (top) andreasnikolas/Shutterstock.com; p. 24 (bottom) James And James/Photodisc/Getty Images; p. 26 © iStockphoto.com/Steve Debenport; p. 28 © iStockphoto.com/andresr; p. 30 Jupiterimages/Pixland/Thinkstock; p. 32 Will & Deni McIntyre/Science Source/Getty Images; p. 34 Roy McMahon/Photodisc/Getty Images; p. 38 © iStockphoto.com/Alex Potemkin; p. 40 Fuse/Corbis/Getty Images; p. 42 © iStockphoto.com/Jason V; p. 47 bluelela/Shutterstock.com; cover and interior pages icons and graphics Shutterstock.com: Anna_leni (owl), Draze Design (pad and pencil), RedlineVector (light bulb), Yuri Gayvoronskiy (eyes), james Weston (scrambled numbers), Ratoca (thumbs up), BeRad (magnifying glass).

Contents

If you work hard and follow the tips in this book, you will soon master math word problems.

Problem-Solving Tips

You may wonder why you have to solve word problems. Word problems come up in lots of situations. You may see them in your homework, on a test, or in your life. These tips can help you solve them, no matter where they turn up.

 ## Be positive!

Look forward to learning something new. You might not get a problem right the first time. That's OK. You know you will be able to figure it out if you stay positive.

 ## It's OK to ask for help!

Teachers, parents, and even friends can be great resources. They want to help you learn. They may help you see a problem in a new way, too.

In some problems, you will see clue spotters. A magnifying glass will help you spy clue words in the problem.

Practice makes perfect!

The more you practice anything, the better you become at it. Homework problems are your practice for word problems.

Move on!

If you run into a problem you are having trouble with, move to the next problem. Do the ones you know how to solve first. You'll feel more confident. And you won't miss the ones you know because you ran out of time. Go back later and try the problems you skipped.

Ask questions!

When someone is helping you, asking good questions tells the person what you don't understand. If you don't ask questions, you will never get answers!

It's OK to take a break!

If you are starting to get frustrated, take a break. Close your eyes and take a deep breath. Stretch. Get a drink of water or a snack. Then come back and try again.

Don't give up!

The first time you try to solve a word problem, you might come up with an answer that does not make sense or that you know is not right. Don't give up! Check your math. Try solving the problem a different way. If you quit, you won't learn.

Problem Solving, Step-by-Step

Word problems can be solved by following four easy steps.

? **Here's the problem.**

Harold's family ordered an extra super deluxe supreme pizza. They ate 1/3 of the pizza in the parking lot and another 1/3 in the car on the way home. In all, how much pizza was eaten before they got home?

Pizza is an easy dinner for a family. It is also a great food for practicing and understanding fractions!

Read and understand the problem.

Step one is to read the problem carefully. Ask yourself questions, like:

What do you know?

They ate 1/3 of the pizza in the parking lot and 1/3 of the pizza in the car.

What are you trying to find?

How much of the pizza they ate before they got home.

What is happening in the problem?

They ate some, then ate some more

Make a plan.

Some problems tell you how they should be solved. For other problems, you need to make your own plan. That's the second step: figure out how you want to solve the problem. Most problems can be solved in more than one way. Some plans you might try are:

Look for a pattern   Write an equation

Draw a picture   Use a model

Estimate   Break it apart

How can you solve this problem?

You can draw a picture.

Solve the problem.

Time for step three: It is time to do the math!

If you find that your plan is not working, make a new plan. Don't give up the first time.

Let's draw a picture.

Draw a circle for the pizza.

This problem uses fractions that are thirds. To show thirds, make 3 equal sections in the circle.

Harold's family ate 1/3 of the pizza in the parking lot.

Shade 1/3 of the circle to show how much they ate.

They ate another 1/3 of the pizza in the car. Shade another 1/3 of the circle to show how much they ate in the car.

How much of the circle is shaded?

Two of the thirds, or 2/3, is shaded.

Harold's family ate 2/3 of the pizza before they got home.

Look back.

The problem is solved!

But you aren't finished yet.

The last step is to take a good look at your answer.

Does it make sense? Did you include the units? Did you use the right numbers to begin? Estimate or use a different operation to check your math.

Is there another way you can solve this problem?

Yes. You can write an addition equation.

1/3 + 1/3 = 2/3

Ways to Solve Word Problems

❗ Use a Picture

Sometimes the answer to a problem is in a picture.

❓ Here's the problem.

Maddie cut 1 muffin into 2 equal parts. Look at the picture. What fraction of the muffin do you see?

This blueberry muffin has been cut into two pieces. We can see one piece clearly in the picture.

Read and understand.

What do you know?

Maddie cut 1 muffin into 2 equal parts.

What are you trying to find?

What fraction of the muffin we see in the picture.

Plan.

Look at the picture to see how much of the muffin is left.

Solve.

There are 2 equal parts in one whole muffin, so 2 is the denominator (bottom number).

From the picture, you can see there is 1 part of muffin visible. Subtract to find how many parts are missing. $2 - 1 = 1$. Maddie must have eaten 1 part of the muffin. One is the number of parts being talked about. It is the numerator (top number). Maddie has eaten $1/2$ of the muffin so far.

Look back.

Does your answer make sense?

Yes, you can see that 1/2 of the muffin is left, so 1/2 is gone.

Fraction Strips

Fraction strips can help you compare fractions.

Here's the problem.

Jenna used $1/4$ of a mango in her fruit smoothie. Jill used $1/3$ of a mango in hers. Who used more mango?

Smoothies are made using yogurt and fruit and can be a healthy breakfast or snack.

Read and understand.

What do you know?

Jenna put 1/4 of a mango in her fruit smoothie.

Jill put 1/3 of a mango in her fruit smoothie.

What are you trying to find?

Who used more mango.

What kind of a problem is this?

You are comparing 1/4 and 1/3.

This is a comparison problem.

Plan.

Let's use fraction strips to compare.

You can make fraction strips by cutting across a sheet of paper, then folding each strip into different numbers of equal parts to show different fractions.

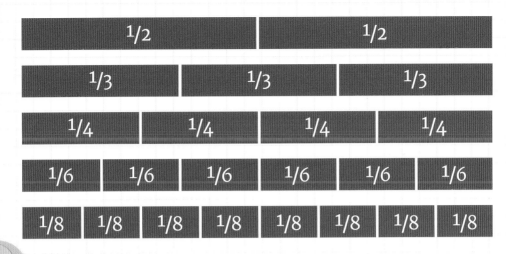

 ## Solve.

Compare the fraction strip for thirds to the fraction strip for fourths.

1/3   1/3   1/3
1/4   1/4   1/4   1/4

Which is longer, 1/3 or 1/4?

1/3 is more than 1/4.

Jill used more mango than Jenna.

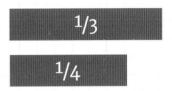

Look back.

Does your answer make sense?

Yes. When there are fewer equal parts in a whole, each part is larger.

A fraction with a numerator (top number) of 1 is called a unit fraction. 1/3 and 1/4 are both unit fractions.

When both numerators are 1, the fraction with the smaller denominator is the larger fraction.

1/3 is larger than 1/4.

More Than One Question

Problems with more than one question need more than one answer.

Here's the problem.

Armand made a 24-inch submarine sandwich and a 12-inch submarine sandwich. He cut each sandwich into 6 equal pieces. What fraction represents 1 piece of a sandwich? Are all 12 pieces the same size?

You could come up with all sorts of fraction problems using a sandwich. For example, you could find out what part of the tomato Armand used on his sandwich or what portion of the cheese he used.

Read and understand.

What do you know?

There are 2 sandwiches. One is 24 inches long. The other is 12 inches long.

14

What are you trying to find?

Two things, a fraction for 1 piece of a sandwich AND if each piece is the same size.

Plan.

Let's draw a picture.

Solve.

Draw a picture. Use an oval or rectangle for each sandwich. Make sure the 24-inch sandwich is twice as long as the 12-inch sandwich. Show 6 equal pieces in each sandwich.

Now answer both questions.

What fraction represents one piece of a sandwich?

One piece is 1/6 of a whole sandwich.

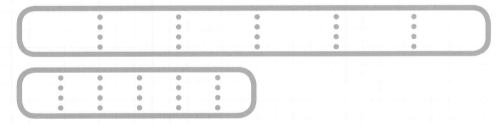

Are all 12 pieces the same size?

No. Pieces of the bigger sandwich are bigger than pieces of the smaller sandwich.

Look back.

Is 1/6 of a sandwich always the same size? No. The size of a fraction of the sandwich depends on the size of the whole sandwich.

Use a Model

You can use items, such as beans, sugar cubes, or pretzel sticks, to model a problem. Or you can use models on paper, such as number lines, diagrams, or graphs.

Here's the problem.

Timmy gave his brother 1/2 a bag of sour gummy worms. There are 16 worms in a bag. How many worms did Timmy give his brother?

Gummy worms and other gummy candies are made with gelatin. The first gummy candies were made in Germany.

Read and understand.

What do you know?

There are 16 gummy worms in a bag.
Timmy gave his brother 1/2 of the gummy worms.

What are you trying to find?

The number of gummy worms he gave his brother.

Plan.

Let's model the problem with gummy worms.

The fraction 1/2 means 1 out of 2 equal parts. There are 16 sour gummy worms, so put the worms in 2 equal groups. An easy way to do this is to put 1 in each group until you run out. A worm for Timmy, 1 for his brother.

When all of the worms are in groups, how many are in each group? 8.

Timmy gave his brother 8 gummy worms.

 Look back.

What does the fraction mean in this problem?
The fraction in this problem is part of a set.
The bag of gummy worms is a set of 16.
Half of the set is 8 gummy worms.
1/2 of 16 is 8.

Is there another way to solve this problem?
Yes.
You can find half of a number by dividing it by 2.
$16 \div 2 = 8$.

Some Fraction Rules

! More Comparing

When you compare like fractions, you only need to look at the numerator (top number).

? Here's the problem.

Pat and Wanda each had 120 jelly beans. Pat ate $3/8$ of her jelly beans. Wanda ate $5/8$ of her jelly beans.

Who ate **more** jelly beans?

Jelly beans are commonly eaten around Easter time, though they can be eaten any time of year.

 Read and understand.

What do you know?

Pat and Wanda each had the same number of jelly beans.

Pat ate 3/8 of her jelly beans.

Wanda ate 5/8 of her jelly beans.

What are you trying to find?

Who ate more jelly beans.

 ## Plan.

Since each girl started with the same number of jelly beans, you can just compare the fractions.

 ## Solve.

Fractions with the same denominator are called like fractions. To compare like fractions, compare the numerators.

3	numerators	5
8	denominators	8

Since 3 is less than 5, 3/8 is less than 5/8.

Wanda ate more jelly beans than Pat.

 ## Look back.

Could you have solved this problem another way? You could draw a picture, or you could use a model like fraction strips.

 # Equivalent Fractions

Fractions that look different can have the same meaning.

Here's the problem.

Hailey and Andria each bought French fries at the fair. Andria put vinegar on 1/4 of her French fries. Hailey put vinegar on 2/8 of her French fries. Hailey said she must like vinegar more than Andria, since she put it on more of her fries. Is she right?

French fries are thinly sliced strips of potato that are generally fried.

 Read and understand.

What do you know?

Andria put vinegar on 1/4 of her French fries.
Hailey put vinegar on 2/8 of her French fries.

What are you trying to find?

Whether Hailey put vinegar on more of her French fries than Andria.

Plan.

Let's use fraction strips to compare.

Find the fraction strips for fourths and eighths.

1/4		1/4		1/4		1/4	
1/8	1/8	1/8	1/8	1/8	1/8	1/8	1/8

Compare 1/4 and 2/8. They are the same. Fractions with the same value are called equivalent fractions.

Hailey is not correct. She and Andria put vinegar on the same amount of French fries.

Look back.

Did you answer the right question?
Yes.

Could you have solved this problem another way? You could use a different model, such as sets of real French fries.

Simplify

Fractions are in simplest form when the only number both the numerator and denominator can be divided by is 1.

Here's the problem.

Luis cut a pan of brownies into 16 squares. He put gooey fudge frosting on 8 of the squares. Write a fraction in simplest form to show how many brownies had frosting.

You need to understand fractions to bake brownies. Recipes always have fractions in them, telling you how much of each ingredient you need to add.

 Read and understand.

What do you know?

There were 16 brownies.

Luis put frosting on 8 of the brownies.

What are you trying to find?

The fraction of brownies with frosting.

 Plan.

Let's write the fraction first, then simplify it.

 Solve.

The total set of brownies is 16.
This is the denominator.
Part of the set, 8 brownies, has frosting. This is the numerator.

$$\frac{8}{16}$$

To simplify a fraction, divide the numerator and denominator by the same number.

8 and 16 can both be divided by 8.

1/2 of the brownies had frosting.

8 ÷ 8	1
16 ÷ 8	2

Look back.

Did you answer the right question?

Yes

Can you check your answer by solving a different way?

Yes. You can use fraction strips to make sure 1/2 is the same as 8/16.

Clue Words

Clue words can help you figure out how to solve problems.

Here's the problem.

Pia had 1/4 gallon of chocolate ice cream and another 1/4 gallon of peanut butter ice cream. How much ice cream did she have in all?

Versions of ice cream were eaten thousands of years ago in Ancient Greece, China, Persia, and Rome. Today ice cream is generally made from milk or cream and sugar.

Problems that combine values are addition problems. In this problem the clue word "another" tells you to add the amount of peanut butter and chocolate ice cream. Some other clue words for addition are: add, altogether, both, combined, increase, more, plus, sum, and total.

? Here's the problem.

Pia had a total of $1/2$ gallon of ice cream. She ate the $1/4$ gallon that was chocolate, and only the peanut butter ice cream was left. How much of Pia's ice cream was peanut butter?

The girl in this picture has three kinds of ice cream. If there are three scoops in the bowl, what fraction of the total would each flavor be?

Problems that start with some then take some away use subtraction.

In this problem, the clue word "**left**" tells you to subtract the amount of ice cream Pia ate from the amount she started with. Other clue words for subtraction are: **compare**, **difference**, **fewer**, **how much less**, **how many more**, **remain**, **subtract**, and **take away**.

Opposite Problems

Let's look at the facts from the two ice cream problems.

1/4 gallon of ice cream is peanut butter.

1/4 gallon of ice cream is chocolate.

There is $^{1}/_{2}$ gallon of ice cream in all.

Pia ate $^{1}/_{4}$ gallon.

Using these facts, you can write two types of problems.

Addition:

$^{1}/_{4}$ gallon + $^{1}/_{4}$ gallon = $^{2}/_{4}$ gallon = $^{1}/_{2}$ gallon

Subtraction:

$^{1}/_{2}$ gallon − $^{1}/_{4}$ gallon = $^{2}/_{4}$ gallon − $^{1}/_{4}$ gallon = $^{1}/_{4}$ gallon

Because they are related, operations that are opposites sometimes use the same clue words, such as "**and**." Clue words can help you get started, but you need to understand what is happening in the problem.

Equations

Equations use numbers and symbols to write a sentence.

Here's the problem.

Larissa had some fresh farm eggs. First, she scrambled 1/5 of the eggs. Then she made custard with 2/5 of the eggs. What fraction of the eggs did Larissa use altogether?

Chickens lay eggs about once a day. It takes about twenty-six hours for most chickens to form an egg.

Read and understand.

What does the problem tell you?
Larissa scrambled 1/5 of the eggs. Then she made custard with 2/5 of the eggs.

26

What are you trying to find?

What fraction of the eggs Larissa used.

Are there any clue words in the problem?

Yes. The clue word "**altogether**" tells you this is an addition problem.

 Plan.

Let's write an equation. Write an addition equation using the numbers you know.

$1/5$ scrambled $+$ $2/5$ custard $=$ fraction of eggs used

 Solve.

So, you've written your equation, and now you need to solve it. To add like fractions (fractions with the same denominator), add the numerators and keep the same denominator.

$1/5 + 2/5 = 3/5$

Larissa used $3/5$ of the eggs.

 Look back.

Did you start with the right numbers?

Yes.

Is there another way to solve this problem?

Yes, you can draw a picture or use a model.

Equations for Measurements

Units of measure, such as inches, cups, gallons, and pounds, often use fractions.

Here's the problem.

Boris bought 7/8 of a pound of potato salad. He gave his dog 1/8 of a pound, then ate what was left himself. How much potato salad did Boris eat?

A dog of this size would likely eat about 1 ½ cups of food twice a day. How much food would that be? Add the whole numbers, then add the fractions.

Read and understand.

What do you know?

Boris bought 7/8 pound of potato salad.
He gave his dog 1/8 pound of the salad.

What are you trying to find?

How much potato salad Boris ate.

Are there any clue words in the problem?

Yes. The clue word "left" tells you this is a subtraction problem.

Plan.

Let's write an equation.

 Solve.

Use the numbers you know to write a subtraction equation.

7/8 pound − 1/8 pound = amount Boris ate

To subtract like fractions, subtract the numerators and keep the same denominator.

7 − 1 = 6

So the new fraction is 6/8.

Simplify the answer.

Divide the numerator and the denominator by 2.

6 ÷ 2 = 3

8 ÷ 2 = 4

So your new fraction is ¾.

Boris ate 3/4 pound of potato salad.

 Look back.

Did you include the units in the answer?

Yes.

Is the math correct? Use addition to check the answer to a subtraction problem.

3/4 + 1/8 = 6/8 + 1/8 = 7/8 Correct!

Make an Easier Problem

Problems that add or subtract unlike fractions are made easier by changing them to like fractions.

Here's the problem.

Billy made a loaf of banana bread. His dad ate $1/2$ of it by himself as soon as it cooled. Then he ate $1/6$ of it after dinner. How much of the banana bread did Billy's dad eat?

This boy is pouring a pint of milk into his recipe. A pint is equal to two cups.

Read and understand.

What do you know?

Billy's dad ate $1/2$ loaf of banana bread.

Then he ate another $1/6$ loaf of banana bread.

What are you trying to find?

How much banana bread Billy's dad ate in all.

What is happening in the problem?

Billy's dad ate some, then ate some more.

This is an addition problem.

 Plan.

Let's write an addition equation.

 Solve.

Use the numbers you know to write an equation.

1/2 loaf + 1/6 loaf = total Billy's dad ate

1/2 and 1/6 are unlike fractions.

Change them to like fractions, then add.

$$\frac{1 \times 3}{2 \times 3} = \,^3/_6$$

$$^3/_6 + \,^1/_6 = \,^4/_6$$

Simplify the answer. $\dfrac{4 \div 2}{6 \div 2}$

$$= \,^2/_3$$

Billy's dad ate ²/₃ of the loaf of banana bread.

 Look back.

Can you use another way to find an equivalent fraction for ¹/₂?

Yes, use fraction strips.

1/2			1/2		
1/6	1/6	1/6	1/6	1/6	1/6

Tips and Tricks to Help You

Start with 1

You can write a whole number, such as 1, as a fraction.

Here's the problem.

Lily filled $3/10$ of her taco with cheese and the rest with meat. What fraction of her taco was filled with meat?

Tacos are a traditionally Mexican food. Today they are a big favorite everywhere in North America.

Read and understand.

What do you know?

Lily filled 3/10 of her taco with cheese.
Lily filled the rest of her taco with meat.

What are you trying to find?

How much of her taco is filled with meat.

Are there any clue words?

No. Some problems do not use clue words.

What kind of problem is this?

The words "**the rest**" tell you the taco is full. You need to find the difference between a full taco and the part filled with cheese. This is a subtraction problem.

 Plan.

Write a subtraction equation.

 Solve.

Lily has one taco. Start with 1. Subtract the fraction of the taco that is filled with cheese.

The whole number 1 can be written as a fraction by putting the same number in the numerator and denominator.

1 taco − 3/10 filled with cheese = fraction filled with meat

$10/10 − 3/10 = 7/10$

7/10 of Lily's taco is filled with meat.

 Look back.

Check your answer.

Add the fraction of the taco that has cheese and the fraction that has meat.

$3/10 + 7/10 = 10/10$, or 1 full taco

Subtract the numerators. Keep the same denominator.

Break It Apart

You can break problems with more than one step into smaller problems to help you solve them.

 **Here's the problem.**

Anna won't eat peas, but her mother put 1/2 cup of them on her plate. She hid 1/8 cup in her pocket and 1/8 cup under the cushion of her chair. She put another 1/8 cup in the fish tank. How much does she have left to hide under her plate?

Doesn't a 1/2 cup look like a lot of peas? Peas are high in fiber, protein, vitamin A, vitamin B6, vitamin C, vitamin K, phosphorus, magnesium, copper, iron, zinc, and lutein.

Read and understand.

What do you know?

Anna started with 1/2 cup of peas.

34

She hid: 1/8 cup in her pocket

1/8 cup under the chair cushion

1/8 cup in the fish tank.

What are you trying to find?

How much Anna has left to hide under her plate.

 ## Plan.

Let's break this problem into smaller problems.

 ## Solve.

First, add to find how much of the peas Anna hid.

$1/8 + 1/8 + 1/8 = 3/8$

Subtract how much she hid from how much she started with.

$1/2 - 3/8 = ?$

$1/2$ and $3/8$ are unlike fractions.

Change them to like fractions, then subtract.

$$\frac{1 \times 4}{4 \times 4} = 4/8$$

$4/8 - 3/8 = 1/8$

Anna has 1/8 cup of peas left to hide under her plate.

 ## Look back.

Read the question again. **Did you miss any information?**

No.

Hidden Information

Words like "dozen," "triple," and "twice" tell you information you may need to know to solve a problem.

Here's the problem.

Brenna needs 2 $\frac{1}{2}$ dozen doughnuts for her 4-H club. How many doughnuts does Brenna need?

Read and understand.

What do you know?

Brenna needs 2 1/2 dozen doughnuts.

What are you trying to find?

How many doughnuts are in 2 1/2 dozen.

Is there any hidden information?

Yes. You need to know that "dozen" means 12.

Plan.

Let's draw a picture.

Solve.

The number 2 1/2 is a mixed fraction.

It has a whole number part and a fraction part.

Use circles for the doughnuts. Draw the whole number part.

Draw 2 sets of 12 circles.

Draw the fraction part.

There are 12 in 1 dozen, so there are 6 in 1/2 a dozen.

Draw 6 more circles.

Count the number of circles. There are 30.

Brenna needs 30 doughnuts.

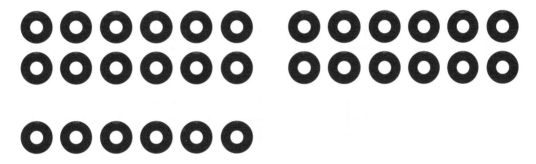

 ## Look back.

Could you have solved this another way?
Yes.

You could have added $12 + 12 + 6 = 30$ or used a model that shows a dozen, like an egg carton.

❗ Use a Number Line

You can use number lines to add, subtract, and compare numbers.

Here's the problem.

Amy's favorite food is souvlaki on pita bread. For lunch, she ate 2 $\frac{1}{2}$ souvlaki pitas. As a snack, she ate another $\frac{1}{2}$ souvlaki pita. How many souvlaki pitas did Amy eat in all?

Souvlaki is a traditional Greek dish served in a pita wrap. Souvlaki can contain meat or vegetables.

Read and understand.

What do you know?

For lunch Amy ate 2 $\frac{1}{2}$ pitas.

She ate another $\frac{1}{2}$ pita as a snack.

What are you trying to find?

How many pitas Amy ate in all.

Are there any clue words in the problem?

Yes. The words "another" tell you this is an addition problem.

Plan.

Let's use a number line to add.

Souvlaki is meat that is cooked on skewers. In Greece, it is a fast food, like a hamburger in America.

Solve.

Amy ate 2 $\frac{1}{2}$ pitas for lunch.

Start at zero. Move right to 2 $\frac{1}{2}$.

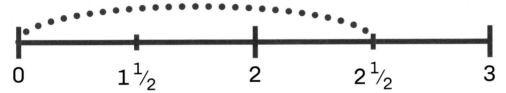

As a snack she ate another $\frac{1}{2}$ pita.

Move right another $\frac{1}{2}$.

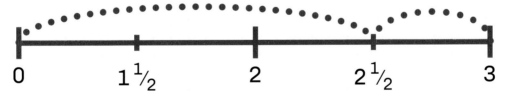

You end at 3.

Amy ate 3 souvlaki pitas in all.

Look back.

Read the problem again. Does your answer match the question?

Yes.

Too Much Information

Too much information can make a problem confusing. You have to think about what is being asked before solving.

Here's the problem.

Jada chopped 6 cups of tomatoes, $3\frac{3}{4}$ cups of green peppers, $1\frac{1}{4}$ cups of hot peppers, and $3\frac{1}{2}$ cups of onions to make salsa. How much more green pepper did she chop than hot pepper?

Recipes tend to use fractions. This is a word problem you want to solve because you want to eat yummy foods!

Read and understand.

What do you know?

Jada chopped: 6 cups of tomatoes

$3\,3/4$ cups of green peppers

$1\frac{1}{4}$ cups of hot peppers

$3\,1/2$ cups of onions

What are you trying to find?

How much more green pepper Jada chopped than hot pepper.

What information do you need to solve the problem?

Since the problem only asks about peppers, underline the amounts of green peppers and hot peppers in the problem.

Plan.

Let's write a subtraction equation.

Solve.

Use the numbers you know to write an equation.

$3\,^3/_4 - 1\,^1/_4 = \text{difference}$

$(\text{green peppers}) - (\text{hot peppers}) = \text{difference}$

$$
\begin{array}{r}
3\ ^3/_4 \\
-1\ ^1/_4 \\
\hline
^2/_4
\end{array}
\qquad
\begin{array}{r}
3\ ^3/_4 \\
-1\ ^1/_4 \\
\hline
2\ ^2/_4 = 2\ ^1/_2
\end{array}
$$

Jada chopped 2 1/2 cups more green peppers than hot peppers.

Look back.

Did you start with the right numbers?

Yes.

Does the answer match the question?

Yes.

First, subtract the fractions.
Then subtract the whole numbers.
Simplify the answer.

Estimation

You can use estimation when you do not need an exact answer or when you want to see if an answer is reasonable.

Here's the problem.

Blake set up a lemonade stand. He sold 3 $\frac{1}{8}$ liters of lemonade the first hour and 4 $\frac{3}{4}$ liters the next hour. About how many liters did he sell in the two hours together?

Lemonade stands can be a great way to make some money in the summer. Don't forget to consider the costs of the supplies, though.

Read and understand.

What do you know?

Blake sold 3 $\frac{1}{8}$ liters of lemonade the first hour.

He sold 4 $\frac{3}{4}$ liters of lemonade the next hour.

What are you trying to find?

About how many liters he sold in the two hours.

 ## Plan.

The question asks about how many liters, not exactly how many.

Let's use estimation to add.

 ## Solve.

Round each mixed fraction to the nearest whole number.

If the fraction part is 1/2 or more, round up to the next whole number.

If the fraction part is less than 1/2, round down.

3 1/8   1/8 is less than 1/2, so round down to 3.

4 3/4   3/4 is more than 1/2, so round up to 5.

Now add the rounded numbers. 3 + 5 = 8

Blake sold about 8 liters of lemonade in the two hours together.

 ## Look back.

Did you start with the right numbers?

Yes.

Did you include the units in your answer?

Yes.

Remember the Plan

To solve a word problem, follow these steps:

Read and understand the problem.

Know what the problem says and what you need to find. If you don't understand, ask questions before you start.

Make a plan.

Choose the plan that makes the most sense and is easiest for you. Remember, there is usually more than one way to find the right answer.

Solve the problem.

Use the plan. If your first plan isn't working, try a different one. Take a break and come back with a fresh mind.

Look back.

Read the problem again. Make sure your answer makes sense. Check your math. If the answer does not look right, don't give up now! Use what you've learned to go back and try the problem again.

Glossary

addition The process of adding two or more numbers together.

denominator The bottom number in a fraction that shows how many equal parts a whole is divided into.

division One of the four basic operations in math; the process of finding out how many times a smaller number is contained within a larger one.

equation A number sentence such as $1 + 1 = 2$, where both expressions on either side of the equals sign are the same.

estimate To make a good guess.

fraction A whole that has been divided into pieces.

inverse The opposite of something else. In math, addition and subtraction are inverses.

multiplication One of the four basic operations in math; the process of repeated addition.

numerator The top number in a fraction that indicates how many parts of a whole we have.

operation A math process, such as addition, subtraction, multiplication, or division.

rounding Using a number that is less exact to help solve problems. For example, 13 would round down to 10 and 17 would round up to 20.

subtraction The process of taking a number away from a larger number.

unit Whatever object is being added or subtracted, such as peppers or pounds of food.

For More Information

Books

Adler, David A. *Working With Fractions.* New York, NY: Holiday House, 2007.

Dodds, Dayle Ann. *Full House: An Invitation to Fractions.* Cambridge, MA: Candlewick Press, 2007.

Websites

Aplusmath
www.aplusmath.com

Interactive math resources for teachers, parents, and students featuring free math worksheets, math games, math flashcards, and more.

Coolmath Games
www.coolmath-games.com

Try your hand at games that make learning and practicing math fun.

Math Playground
www.mathplayground.com/ wordproblems.html

Solve math word problems with Thinking Blocks, Jake and Astro, and more.

Index